Mongrel Prince

Ken Goudsward

ISBN: 978-1-989940-78-5
© 2023 Ken Goudsward
Dimensionfold Publishing
dimensionfold.com

for Sol
& Jeremy
& Raghu
& Res
& Robert

21 jump

my dad was on 21 jump street
with Johnny Depp
as a regularly occurring extra
and it never occurred to him
or he was still too cheap and didn't care
to get cable
to see himself on TV

100 years of shitty memories

they call this a museum
it's what passes in these parts
it's a piece of shit
or rather
a bunch of shit that some farmer left
littered around in the field
or in a forgotten barn corner
it's literally old garbage
from when there were no garbage dumps
because the whole world was the dump
and the mine
and the store
you took whatever you could
find
dig up
kill
rape

these are the best we could come up with
remember our fathers by
those old pieces of shit
look what they did
isn't it something?

A Crust For Chris

Carb free Costco cauliflower crust.
Can you top it?
'course I can!

The sauce is included, just spread it on. Right to the
edges.
A light sprinkling of cheese makes a base layer
Helps it all stick
I used to work at a pizza shop you know
Two actually. Yes, at the same time — don't tell the
bosses.

Now go ahead and add the meat.
Pepperoni, salami,
Forget about ham. That's just a myth. Pineapple goes
with all kinds of meat.

Onions, red pepper
A bit of spinach
And of course the pineapple.
Do not be fooled. This is your only opportunity.

Now a glorious pile of shredded mozzarella
What could be better?
Nothing, I tell you.
It can't be topped!

A million Buffalo

A million Buffalo
Have shaped this land
Eaten the grasses
Melted the ice

A herd
Ten thousand strong
Has been forced by hunters
To run off a cliff
Smashing in their heads
Upon one another

One Buffalo
Keeps trampling me
At regular intervals
I can never tell if it's the same one
For they all look the same to me

A terrible place

Be good they told me
Or you might find
Yourself
Somewhere terrible
A place of eternal
Torment
Like maybe
Winnipeg

become

i have been father
i have been priest
prince prophet
healer teacher lord & slave
mage mystic

Now I am storyteller
Now I become all things

belief

belief is a necessary framework
a set of assumptions
required each morning
to make sense
of the crazy act of existing
that allows me to step outside my door
instead of spending all day
attempting in vain to understand everything

belief is of necessity
a simplification
a boiling down
an extraction
it is merely a model of reality
it is not the thing itself

belief gives me sanity
and hope
and common ground
belief is culture
belief provides community
and communication

belief fuels idealism
ideology, and idea
belief provides identity and identifiers
belief proves identity

belief is the tiny box
that I think I can cram the universe into
and hope that it does not
come springing out
to slap me in the face
or blow me to smithereens

Doctrin

Big Pharma
the doc is on the take
addictive cure from what?
100mg of scripture
is my prescription

Does the Pope shit in the woods?

Does the Pope shit in the woods?
Or in his hat
I dunno
But I guess it would be easy enough to find out
You just gotta
Invite him camping

False prophets

if the thing follow not, nor come to pass
that prophet shall die
thou shalt not be afraid

and they shall see the Son of man coming in the clouds
of heaven with power and great glory.
this generation shall not pass, till all these things be
fulfilled

a good tree cannot bring forth evil fruit

the prophets prophesy falsely,
and the priests bear rule by their means;
and my people love to have it so:
and what will ye do in the end thereof?

for wheresoever the carcass is,
there will the eagles be gathered together.

Fantastic Mundane - #1

I want to be rich
Because I want to retire
Because I want to do my own projects
So why not just do the fucking projects?

I wish people would buy my shit
But why should they?
Why should I need them to?

I want to fucking rock and roll
I wish I could shred
and have killer tone
but I can't and don't
And no one gives a shit
Because it's good enough
         for me
and frankly it does rock

I hope people will buy my novel
and recognize my quality writing
but perhaps it is enough
for it to be
my favorite book

I wish I was a time-traveler, a wizard
I wish I was an amazing lover
I wish I was a good person
but if I were
would I even care?

father hood

i have been called both
"hood", "father"
or to be more precise, "dad"
and "pop-pop"

and when i read poetry
sometimes at least i
become convinced that he is talking
about me

that i am the source
of all pain
the source of
all names

i know
it was my idiocy
that caused tears
heartbreak becomes a cycle

and it is thus
that makes me want to die
that forces me to go on living

fire #1

a fire is not a thing
a molecule
also not a thing really
but let's pretend
for now
gets hot
and its rate of oxidation increases
so that carbon atom
for example
also not a thing
breaks off
to join up with oxygen instead
which is very exciting
for both of them
and gives off energy
which heats up their neighbors
it's contagious
the surrounding air
heats up
rises
vacates
creates vacuum
pulls them up
and this air takes some of their heat
and it gets so hot that
it releases photons
which
to me and you
looks like fire

fire #2

such fearsome power
for a thing that
is not even a thing
really,
just plasma which
like me
is fleeing the heat
avoiding the reaction
and spreading
their social charge

fire #3

life
the collection
the explosion
devouring all in its path
and shitting it out the other end

has engulfed this planet
and uncountable others
just wait til it gets going

Fried

Hand picked
Hand sorted
Hand washed
Hand delivered
Hand cut

Boiled in golden oil
Salted
And served up
(In a cute little cardboard basket)

Here I sit
At the right hand of
Burger Royale

garbage

what is this?
an obsolete connector. an outdated textbook. clothes I
never wear.
is it garbage?
can it be garbage?

I can choose
my label doesn't negate the value it held
it merely pins it into the past

why keep it?
now it becomes a burden
no present use
at least not for me

throw it out
making room for the future.

Government Grants

Well, I was serious, but…
If R. Keith is marginal and Guitar Smashing is out,
I'm afraid I don't know grantable
from a hole
in the ground
…thus
I shall back away slowly
whistling a baleful melody

handles have baggage

Poems label concepts
Conceptualize labels
Complex forms
Structural entities
These are weighty
Too large to drag around
The label is a name
Perhaps a description
Maybe a few instructions
If we are lucky
But it is misleading
It fails to encompass, encapsulate
The transitive nature
The transition to nature
To mature transfer and transcend
The label
 the concepts
The word is a handful
A handle
To leverage the thought
But handles have baggage

hardy har har

you are just too funny
aren't you?

healing

perhaps
the healing of Christ
is the healing from Christ

Hey buddy, wanna buy a chapbook?

yeah
I didn't think so
well fuck you

i don't think this computer is very good

it sucks
my time, mostly
seriously
five minutes to boot up
like what the fuck man

but it's the one I have
not the best one I have
but the one I can legitimately use
the one I own

if one can own a thing
or does the thing own you?
sometimes it sure
feels like it

it feels like owning me
so it goes extra slow
that son of a bitch
it thinks it controls me
I suppose it is right

just words

this is where a poem would go
were i a poet
or where i would bare my soul
were i an honest man
but for now
it is just words

this page should hold something great
something indicative
something poignant
but
it is just words

it should speak of love
of longing
of sadness, grief, anger, and disillusionment
and of unrealistic expectations and shattered hopes
it should convey helpless gratitude
in waves big enough to sink Tokyo
and joy piled up to the clouds
but it doesn't
and i can not
my heart does not contain or comprehend these feelings
it is just words

Kelowna 2020

I sat
on an bench
in the mall
in Kelowna
that day
the day of the outbreak
and I didn't even buy any chocolates
I just sat and edited some poetry
written by a great man
my son
and, inspired
wrote several poems myself
while all around
sparsely
people shopping
throwing axes
not the typical busy foot traffic
and some were infected I guess
but I didn't touch any of them
at least not in that way
and at least not yet

Kelowna 2021

One year later
Again sitting in the mall
This time I did the unthinkable
And actually bought
myself some clothes
But
Still the wildfires burn
Still the pandemic rages
So I write another poem
What else can I do?

Leave off!

Leave off!
My mind is not small
My memory is not small
My feelings are not small
My ideas are not small
My name is not small
My heart is not small
My spirit is not small
My world is not small

Meat and Greet

meat and greet
hello friend
how have you been?

meet and grit
not too bad, thanks
(now go away)

mete and great
divided we climb
with cleavers and levers

mate and grate
a nightcap?
(or a nightmare)

Mighty Men of Old

Enoch and Noah
And Jesus and Tesla
Walk into a bar
Pints of mead all around
They have a good chat
They zap each other with lightning bolts
It's all in good fun
Into the bar walks the Buddha
Oh, there you guys are
Why didn't you wait for me?

Moses

Moses
Was the Pharaoh
That everybody hated
With his one true Aten
His cute little family
And their beautiful kittens
Their servants fanning them
As they reclined along the river bank
But he had the last laugh
Hovering above Mount Sinai
That Sapphire throne
This golden rod
Keep in touch he said
And don't go making Golden calves

Nieces and Nephews

Nieces and Nephews
Are driving into town
Are getting evicted
Are buying a new shirt
Are eating maple bacon chips
Are telling me
About the Edmonton Oilers
And about the six best video games
That I will buy for them
When I win the lottery

Ocean of lies

He walks upon the water
He calms the raging seas
He hovers upon
the face of the deep
the puddles of mystery
the ocean of lies

Pretzels

There's gotta be a pretzel stand
Around here
You know the one I mean
It's got garlic and parmesan and herbs
And it feels like pure joy
Like sunshine and sex
And bass solos
And brand new chapbooks
If all those things were made out of bread

But no
Apparently there isn't one
How can it be?
We even have one back home in P.G.!

sExistentialism

Why are we here
With these penises and vaginas
With these testicles, breasts, eyes
"I"s
"We"s
We shall sees
We shall seize
A seizure
A spasm

stamp

the church can not be stamped out
for its fire will only grow more fervent
it must be choked out
not with bare hands
but with a plastic bag
asphyxiation is the only way
to allow a fresh breath

the church must be stamped out
using a cookie cutter
it must be baked and cooled
naked and cool
deprived of fig leaves
anointed with olive oil
and left to dry
perhaps to rediscover its salt

Standing in the lobby

Standing in the lobby
Bank of Montreal
Mount royal
     high and mighty
     steep sided
Royal bank
     banks of the royal river
     the mighty flow
          sweeps all down
     the slippery slope
Royal stank
     the air thick (like his wallet)(and the vault door)
Royal frank
     makes no bones - made of pigs feet
Royal tank
     it will run you over for oil
Royal ankh
she waits in this temple
desperate for a lifegiving drop
a meagre peasant
no one
waiting for your refusal
your denial

states

orgasm is state
rather than event
enter and exit at will

peace/pleasure/joy/beauty/awe
is state
rather than response
enter and exit at will

organism is state
rather than individual
no exit
from this communist democracy

organs/institutions are stateful
are born into involuntarily
not merely an anarcho-syndicalist collective of cells
whose opinions and complaints may be felt
higher up
but what of their votes
and who is this higher up anyway?

the collective consciousness
the shared subconscious
the zeitgeist
the state that experiences the state
the orgasm, the awe, the complaints of the organs
was it elected?
does it enter and exit by will?
is it state, event, response, or individual?

streams

of consciousness
they said
yeah, right
as if we are conscious
and as if there's a stream of anything
more like mud puddles of meh

Suits

suits
for weddings and
for bathing
but definitely not for your birthday

The Apostle Paul

The Apostle Paul
Is overcompensating
He drives a huge
Jacked-up F250
With knobby tires
And rolling coal as he
Squeals into the Walmart
Parking lot
Where he says his peace
Before gettin
Run outta town
On a rail

The DNA of gods

The DNA of gods
And of monsters
Of Neanderthal
And octopus
Runs blue in my veins
Runs red for the hills
The high places
Where angels land
To tell of broken promises
And absent priestesses

The skeleton

The skeleton
Is behind bars
But they are only lines
Of latitude
I suppose he will be alright
He is from the north

The thurisaz

The thurisaz
Rides upon a pair of crows
Named Urim and Thummim
They feed the prophet Elijah
While he writes love letters to Odin
His staff and his ankh
Will comfort me
In the prescience of my friends
And I will ride the lightning
Unto the ends of the earth

The year I learned to Ollie

It was 2017
I dug out my old Powell Peralta
Tony Hawk concave
Vert Ramp board
From 1980.. I wanna say… seven?

My kids had pretty much all grown up
I quit Church
I had some time on my hands

So yeah This was it
This was my chance
You tube would show me the way
I had this
I was going to get air

So I'm out on the road
Fucking Gogolin Road
Fucking Peden Hill bitches!
Tony Hawk and you tube
Will be my salvation

"Just slide your foot," They said
Sure
How exactly does sliding one's foot defy the force of
gravity?
It fucking doesn't man!
You tube is a fucking joke
So I sold my skateboard

This book is the only one of its kind

This book is the only one of its kind
which is to say
the only one exactly like it
with these exact poems
with this exact poem
big freaking deal

Three sightings

The first time
That I saw a UFO
It was very high
A small dot
Way up there
But there aren't any flight paths that just go straight over
Prince George
Are there?
Oh
China to Toronto eh?
Ok then

The second time
Was at night
It looked like a small star
But there weren't any other stars
Out yet
And it seemed to move slightly
Didn't it?
Didn't it?
Maybe not

The third time
I didn't even see it
Not really
Not directly
I only saw it's triple beaming
Lights glaring through
My barren window
That faced the lake

47

Silently
Waking me
And when I jumped out
Of bed
There were no boats
Who goes boating at night anyway?

To be or not to be

what kind of question is that?
rhetorical?
maybe not
i can't tell
please do not ask

Uterine

Uterine
Uterout
Uterus
Uterthem

You're In
Tear it out
We all know
They are the enemy

wake

wound down
dark rain white noise
murmur hers
floats upon foam
pale facade
before the curtain
and the sliding image
redundant fractal fracture
eliminates assumptions
proves an archetype
that I just kept
waiting for

Weddings and funerals

Weddings and funerals
Will be taking place
Have taken place
Taking our place
In that cycle
That structure
I based everything I know on it

West end girls

West end girls
Are walking past
I only see their shoes
And the murmur of a thousand
Languages and lands
I feel a bit sad for them
Cuz they had to go across that bridge
The one we took yesterday
And that traffic is brutal

what exactly is my general fucking problem?

what exactly is my general fucking problem?
I ask myself
and I suddenly find it odd that no one else has bothered
to ask me
and maybe that IS part of the problem
cuz I'm a bit of an asshole
and that type of thing should not just go under the radar
like that
it's actually not OK
that we are all assholes
(present company excepted, dear reader)

so what exactly is my general fucking problem?
I guess I'm frustrated
I feel stressed
cuz I can't do what i want
but not in a childish way
like i want to just do whatever i want whenever I want
but that I can only ever seem to make slow progress
like I can do, but never get done
the real things i really want
the things that make me me
and that when i do finally get a chance to work on them
I lack the energy to do it
cuz I already spend all day doing fucking useless shit
or maybe it wasn't totally useless
maybe it helped somebody with their goals
but it didn't help me with my goals
so i squeeze in this work - my real work
wherever I can

but it's not enough
it takes so long
and I'm not fully convinced
that I actually enjoy it
or that i even want to do it

and I'm stressed and irritated and mad as hell
at the bullshit that surrounds me
the idiotic decisions
the sheer incompetence,
ignorance, laziness, and
general sabotage of anything decent
and maybe this IS hell

but it really isn't my problem
it's not like there's anything I can do
and I know that
but i can't seem to break free of it
I can't let it go
and maybe THIS is hell
the real problem lies within
it is the failure to accept
that the problem lies without
that it has nothing to do with me
and therefore everything to do with me
as if I am the very nature of the problem
and that maybe I am hell

for to err is human
and to be an asshole is human
and to be a complete fucking retard is human

and yet this humanity is the divine image
and that heaven is within us
and that to attempt to become an empty shell
is an exercise in futility
and completely defeats the point
of living
and then I wonder why we bother
living at all
but dying seems too extreme
and this grey area in between life and death
is completely intolerable

Wise Guys

In my dad's defence
Around that same time
I was also an extra
In a couple of shows
And I don't even know their names
That's just how it was in hollywood north
You were there for the twenty bucks or whatever
I recall only that one of them
Was called Wise Guys
Or else Wiseguy
Or something like that
And we had to wear black
For a crowded outdoor funeral
And I never saw it
Or heard about its release
And I'm not even sure if it was a film
Or a tv series
A generations later, my son
Saw a film that he thought might have been it
But it didn't have an outdoor funeral scene

www.ingramcontent.com/pod-product-compliance
Lightning Source LLC
Chambersburg PA
CBHW021913040426
42447CB00007B/832